# My State
# NEW HAMPSHIRE

By Christina Earley



## TABLE OF CONTENTS

New Hampshire. . . . . . . . . . . . . . . . 3
Glossary . . . . . . . . . . . . . . . . . . . . . . 22
Index . . . . . . . . . . . . . . . . . . . . . . . . . 24

A Crabtree Seedlings Book

Crabtree Publishing
crabtreebooks.com

# School-to-Home Support for Caregivers and Teachers

This book helps children grow by letting them practice reading. Here are a few guiding questions to help the reader build his or her comprehension skills. Possible answers appear in red.

## Before Reading:

- What do I know about New Hampshire?
    - *I know that New Hampshire is a state.*
    - *I know that New Hampshire is in the northeastern United States.*

- What do I want to learn about New Hampshire?
    - *I want to learn which famous people were born in New Hampshire.*
    - *I want to learn what the state flag looks like.*

## During Reading:

- What have I learned so far?
    - *I have learned that Concord is the state capital of New Hampshire.*
    - *I have learned that the Presidential Range is a mountain range in White Mountain National Forest.*

- I wonder why...
    - *I wonder why the state flower is the purple lilac.*
    - *I wonder why New Hampshire makes so much maple syrup.*

## After Reading:

- What did I learn about New Hampshire?
    - *I have learned that you can swim at Hampton Beach State Park.*
    - *I have learned that the state animal is the white-tailed deer.*

- Read the book again and look for the glossary words.
    - *I see the word **capital** on page 6, and the word **seal** on page 12. The other glossary words are found on pages 22 and 23.*

NEW HAMPSHIRE
Hi! My name is Max. Welcome to New Hampshire!

I live in Portsmouth. It is a **seaport**.

Some buildings in my city were built in the 1600s!

New Hampshire is in the northeastern United States. The **capital** is Concord.

Fun Fact: Manchester is the largest city in New Hampshire.

The state animal is the white-tailed deer.

The purple lilac is
the state flower.

We make a lot of maple syrup in New Hampshire. Most of it is used for pancakes.

Fun Fact: New Hampshire **produces** around 160,000 gallons (606,000 liters) of maple syrup a year.

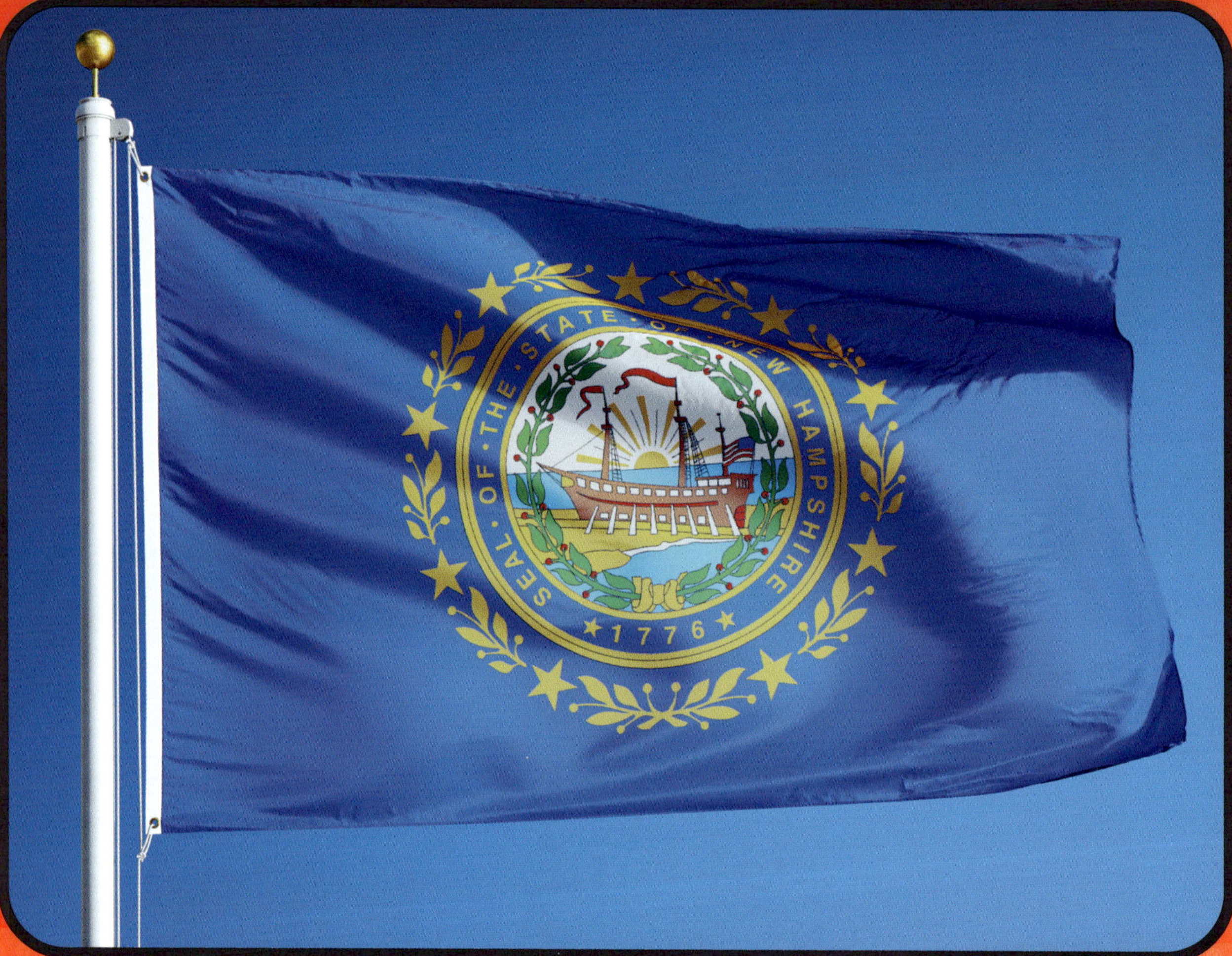


My state flag is blue. The state **seal** is in the middle.

I like to see the **historic** buildings at Canterbury Shaker Village.

I like to visit White Mountain National Forest. Sometimes I see bald eagles.

Fun Fact: The Presidential Range is a group of 13 mountains, many of which are named after U.S. presidents.

I like to go snowshoeing with my family on Table Rock trail.

Cruising Lake Winnipesaukee on a **paddleboat** is relaxing.

Astronaut Alan Shepard was born in New Hampshire. Actress and singer Mandy Moore was also born in New Hampshire.

Fun Fact: President Franklin Pierce was born in Hillsboro, New Hampshire.

Hampton Beach State Park is my favorite place to swim.

I enjoy canoeing along the Northern Forest Canoe Trail.

# Glossary

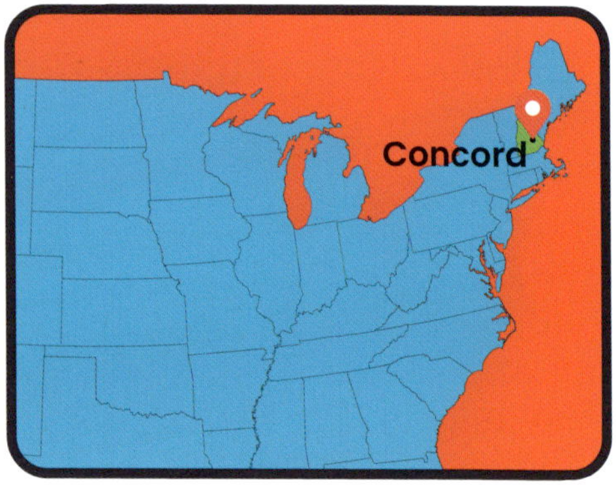


**capital** (cap-ih-tuhl): The city or town where the government of a country, state, or province is located

**historic** (hi-stor-ik): Something that is important in history

**paddleboat** (pad-uhl-boht): A small boat with paddle wheels that are turned by pedals

**produces** (pruh-doos-es): Makes or grows something for sale or use

**seal** (seel): A special design that is used on important papers and other items

**seaport** (see-pohrt): A town or city with a harbor that is used by ships to load and unload cargo

## Index


Concord 6

Hampton Beach State Park 20

Lake Winnipesaukee 17

Moore, Mandy 18

purple lilac 9

Table Rock trail 16


## About the Author

Christina Earley lives in sunny South Florida with her husband and son. She enjoys traveling around the United States and learning about different historical places. Her hobbies include hiking, yoga, and baking.

Written by: Christina Earley

Designed and Illustrated by: Bobbie Houser

Series Development: James Earley

Proofreader: Melissa Boyce

Educational Consultant: Marie Lemke M.Ed.

Photographs:
NASA: p. 18 left
Shutterstock: Jon Bilous: cover; Jon Bilous: p. 3; Wangkun Jia: p. 4, 20, 23; Wangkun Jia: p. 5; Volina: p. 6, 22; Sean Pavone: p. 7; Michael Sean OLeary: p. 8; freya-photographer: p. 9; meunierd: p. 10-11; Andrew Cline: p. 11, 23; railway fx: p. 12, 23; Jeffrey M. Frank: p. 13, 22; Winston Tan: p. 14-15; drewthehobbit: p. 15; ChiccoDodiFC: p. 16; Paul Vasarhelyi: p. 17, 22; DFree: p. 18 right; Anastasia Tveretinova: p. 21
whitehouse.gov: p. 19

**Crabtree Publishing**

crabtreebooks.com 800-387-7650





Printed in the U.S.A./072023/CG20230214

**Published in Canada**
**Crabtree Publishing**
616 Welland Avenue
St. Catharines, Ontario
L2M 5V6

**Published in the United States**
**Crabtree Publishing**
347 Fifth Avenue
Suite 1402-145
New York, New York, 10016

**Library and Archives Canada Cataloguing in Publication**
Available at Library and Archives Canada

**Library of Congress Cataloging-in-Publication Data**
Available at the Library of Congress

Hardcover: 978-1-0398-0526-2
Paperback: 978-1-0398-0558-3
Ebook (pdf): 978-1-0398-0622-1
Epub: 978-1-0398-0590-3